GEMSTONES OF THE WORLD

TUNNELING FOR TURQUOISE

TANYA DELLACCIO

PowerKiDS press.

New York

Published in 2018 by The Rosen Publishing Group, Inc.
29 East 21st Street, New York, NY 10010

Copyright © 2018 by The Rosen Publishing Group, Inc.

First Edition

Editor: Theresa Morlock
Book Design: Reann Nye

Photo Credits: Cover wiiz/Shutterstock.com; p. 4 De Agostini / A. Dagli Orti/ De Agostini Picture Library/Getty Images; p. 5 Reid Dalland/Shutterstock.com; pp. 6, 9 (bottom), 10, 11, 14, 18 vvoe/Shutterstock.com; p. 7 aregfly/Shutterstock.com; p. 8 bigjom jom/Shutterstock.com; p. 9 (top) Nastya Pirieva/Shutterstock.com; p. 12 Fotosoroka/Shutterstock.com; p. 13 underworld/Shutterstock.com; p. 15 Danita Delimont/Gallo Images/Getty Images; p. 16 ruzanna/Shutterstock.com; p. 17 Paula Bronstein/Getty Images News/Getty Images; p. 19 Michael Lynch/EyeEm/Getty Images; p. 20 Junjira Limcharoen/Shutterstock.com; p. 21 Hannes Magerstaedt/Getty Images Entertainment/Getty Images; p. 22 Vereschagin/Shutterstock.com.

Cataloging-in-Publication Data

Names: Dellaccio, Tanya.
Title: Tunneling for turquoise / Tanya Dellaccio.
Description: New York : PowerKids Press, 2018. | Series: Gemstones of the world | Includes index.
Identifiers: LCCN ISBN 9781538328316 (pbk.) | ISBN 9781508164180 (library bound) | ISBN 9781538328378 (6 pack)
Subjects: LCSH: Turquoise–Juvenile literature. | Mineralogy–Juvenile literature.
Classification: LCC QE394.T8 D39 2018 | DDC 553.8'7–dc23

Manufactured in the United States of America

CPSIA Compliance Information: Batch Batch #BW18PK: For Further Information contact Rosen Publishing, New York, New York at 1-800-237-9932

CONTENTS

UNIQUE BEAUTY 4

MAKING MINERALS 6

WHAT'S A MATRIX? 10

FEATURES OF TURQUOISE 12

WHERE DOES IT COME FROM? 16

HOW IS IT MINED? 18

TURQUOISE TREASURES 20

TERRIFIC TURQUOISE 22

GLOSSARY 23

INDEX 24

WEBSITES 24

UNIQUE BEAUTY

Turquoise is a striking bluish-green gemstone. It's almost always opaque, which means you can't see through it.

For thousands of years, turquoise has been prized for its **unique** beauty. Ancient Egyptians used the gemstone to decorate their most important belongings. Some American Indian peoples use turquoise to create **jewelry** and other decorative and **ceremonial** objects. Historically, the Aztec people used turquoise in sculptures representing their gods. Today, people continue to use turquoise to create eye-catching artwork and jewelry.

HIDDEN GEMS

Decorative objects featuring turquoise, such as this piece of jewelry from Tibet, have been found all over the world.

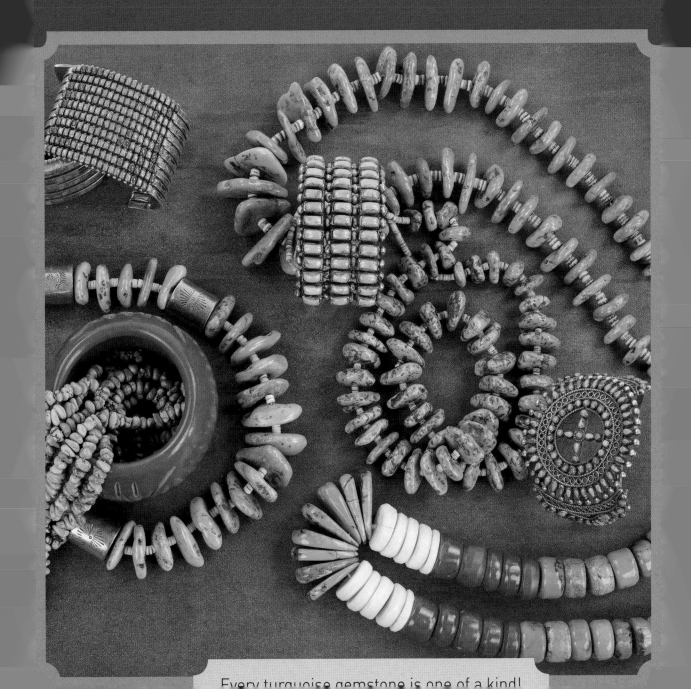

Every turquoise gemstone is one of a kind!

MAKING MINERALS

Sediment is small pieces of gravel, sand, or rocks carried by wind or water. When layers of sediment settle and become pressed together over time, sedimentary rocks form. Turquoise often forms in sedimentary rocks.

Turquoise is a mineral. Minerals are solid natural **substances** that don't come from plants, animals, or other living things. They're formed through natural processes. Minerals are made up of chemical elements. These elements join together and are arranged in a certain way.

HIDDEN GEMS

The amount of copper, phosphorus, and aluminum that are present affect the color of the gemstone.

Turquoise is made up of the elements phosphorus, copper, and aluminum.

Turquoise is usually formed in arid, or hot and dry, places. In these areas, rain flows down through soil and rock, collecting copper as it goes. Over time, the water carrying the copper **evaporates**, leaving the element behind. In rocks where the copper mixes with phosphorus and aluminum, turquoise is formed.

The combination of copper, phosphorus, and aluminum causes crystals to grow. Turquoise may form in veins through sedimentary rocks or in clumps. It sometimes appears as an aggregate, or group, of small crystals.

The amount of copper in turquoise affects how blue it is.

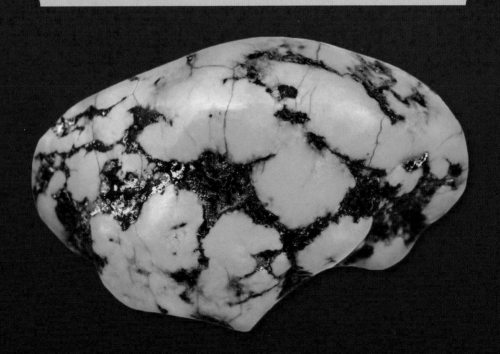

9

WHAT'S A MATRIX?

The host rock may leave behind pieces and markings within a turquoise stone. These are known as a matrix. Matrices appear as black or brown patterns in the gemstone. These patterns are often weblike. Though some people prefer turquoise with these patterns, gemstones with matrices are considered less valuable than those without.

Solid-colored turquoise without imperfections is given the highest value. Robin's-egg blue, a bright, light blue color, is the most popular shade of turquoise.

Iran is famous for producing turquoise that is robin's-egg blue.

FEATURES OF TURQUOISE

Gemstones are sorted based on their features, including **transparency** and hardness. Turquoise is one of the most popular opaque gemstones.

Turquoise is a fairly soft mineral. It's about a 5 on the Mohs' scale. The Mohs' scale measures a mineral's hardness based on how **resistant** it is to being scratched. Diamonds are a 10 on the scale, meaning that they're the hardest mineral. At a 5 on the scale, turquoise is soft enough to carve and shape easily.

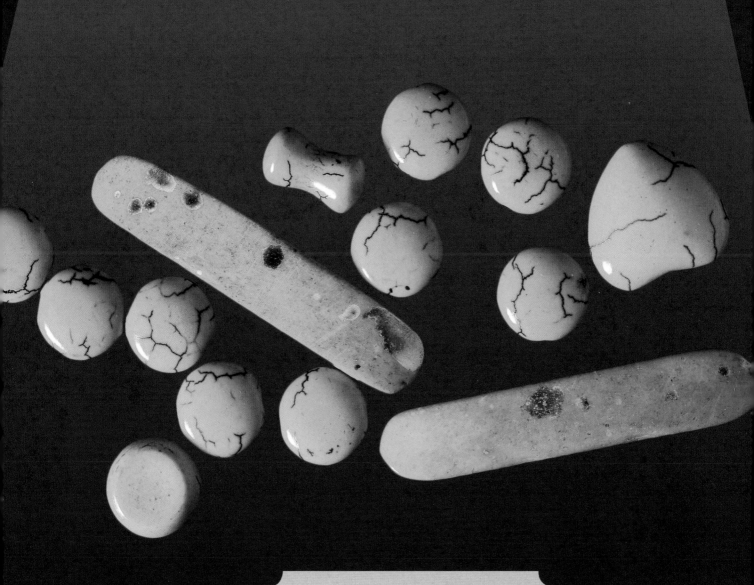

Gemstones that are shaped and
polished but not faceted, or cut,
are called cabochons.

Turquoise is porous. That means it has tiny spaces and holes in it through which water and air can pass. A stone that's too porous may weaken and break. Turquoise is often coated with a substance to make it stronger. In its natural form turquoise has a waxy appearance. Coating turquoise may make it shinier.

Turquoise's unique color makes it highly sought after. However, turquoise may be dyed to change or brighten its color. Because it's porous, turquoise absorbs, or takes in, liquids such as dye.

Since turquoise gemstones can be soft and breakable, they're often treated before they're sold.

15

Turquoise **deposits** can be found throughout the southwestern United States, including Arizona, Colorado, New Mexico, California, Nevada, and Utah. Turquoise can also be found in Nishapur, Iran; the Sinai Peninsula, Egypt; Eilat, Israel; and parts of Mexico.

Turquoise is referred to by different names in different places. The word "turquoise" means "Turkish stone." Europeans used this name because the stone was shipped to Europe through Turkey. The ancient Romans called turquoise "callaïs" and the Aztecs called it "chalchihuitl."

HIDDEN GEMS

Today, the United States is the world's largest producer of turquoise.

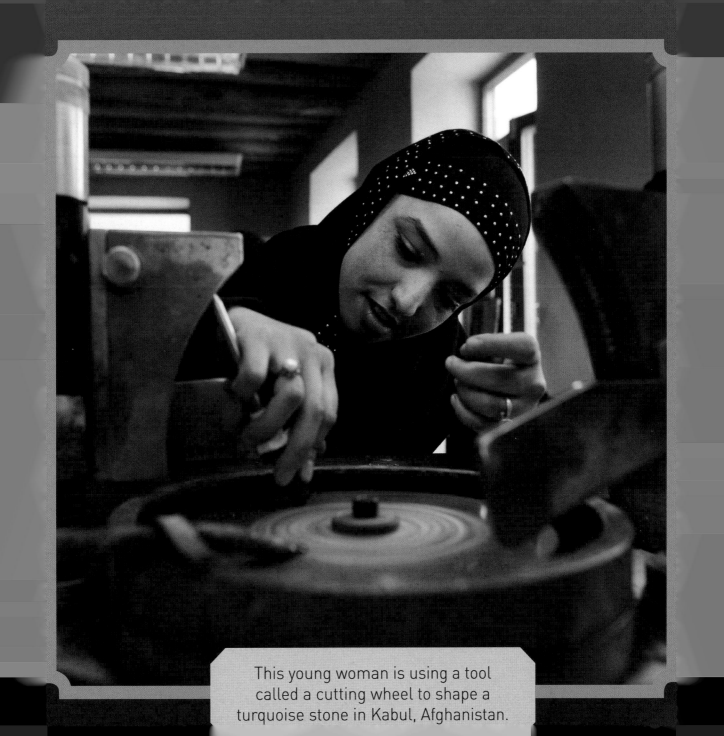

This young woman is using a tool called a cutting wheel to shape a turquoise stone in Kabul, Afghanistan.

HOW IS IT MINED?

Turquoise is often mined at copper mining sites. Since copper is part of turquoise, turquoise gemstones can usually be found in rocks near copper deposits.

Turquoise may be extracted, or taken out, from the host rock carefully using hand tools such as shovels, picks, or hammers. Large veins of turquoise may be extracted using big machinery and are later sorted out of the host rock. After turquoise is extracted, it's cut and treated to be used in jewelry.

MAGNESITE

HIDDEN GEMS

Howlite and magnesite are light-colored minerals that are sometimes dyed and sold as turquoise! These dyed stones aren't as valuable as real turquoise. Buyers must take care to make sure they're buying real turquoise and not look-alikes.

Turquoise is usually found near copper deposits, like Bingham Canyon mine in Utah.

TURQUOISE TREASURES

The earliest-known use of turquoise was in Egypt, over 6,000 years ago. The Egyptians created beautiful turquoise jewelry and ornaments, which were buried with pharaohs, or rulers. Tutankhamen's famous golden funeral mask featured turquoise **inlays**. His sarcophagus, or coffin, was also covered in turquoise.

An Aztec **mosaic** of a two-headed serpent that dates back to the 16th century is made almost entirely of turquoise pieces. The serpent was probably used to represent an Aztec god. The piece was most likely worn during religious ceremonies.

HIDDEN GEMS

Turquoise is an important gemstone to the Navajo Indians. It's used for jewelry and religious ceremonies. Many believe it represents happiness, health, and luck.

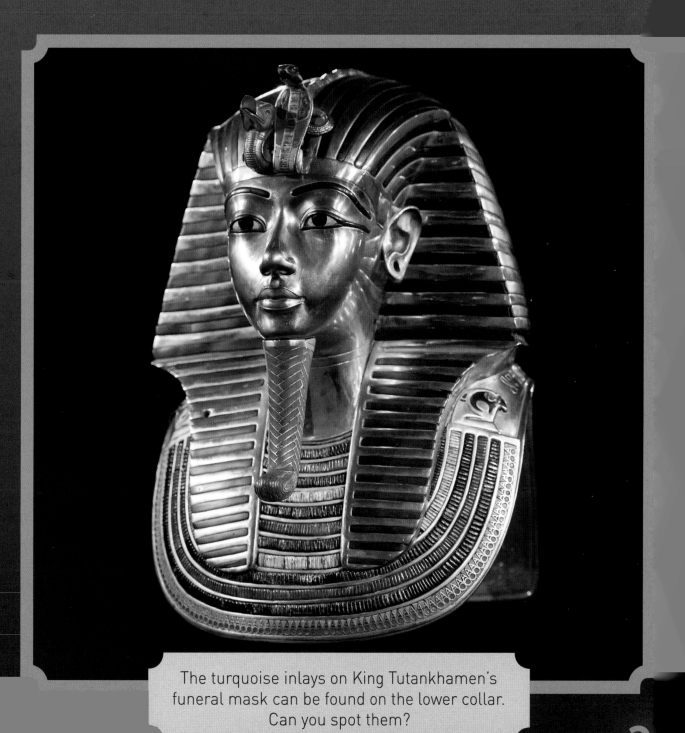

The turquoise inlays on King Tutankhamen's
funeral mask can be found on the lower collar.
Can you spot them?

TERRIFIC TURQUOISE

Historically, many people believed turquoise to have special powers and meaning. The blue of the turquoise is said to represent the sky and the green to represent the earth. Some think that it has healing properties and others believe that it can guard against evil.

From 6,000 years ago to today, this unique and beautiful gemstone has been featured in many important religious objects around the world. Its special blue-green color and opaque appearance make it a favorite of gem fans everywhere.

GLOSSARY

ceremonial: Having to do with a ceremony, or a formal act or event that's part of a social or religious occasion.

deposit: An amount of matter built up naturally in the earth.

evaporate: To change from a liquid to a gas.

inlay: A substance set into a surface of another substance; also, to set pieces of a substance into the surface of something for decoration.

jewelry: Objects people wear on their body for decoration, often made of special metals or prized stones.

mosaic: A decoration made by inlaying small pieces of colored material to form pictures or patterns.

resistant: Able to withstand something.

substance: A kind of material, or something from which something else can be made.

transparency: The degree to which something can be seen through.

unique: Special or different from anything else.

INDEX

A

Afghanistan, 17
aluminum, 6, 7, 8
American Indians, 4
Arizona, 16
Aztecs, 4, 16, 20

C

cabochons, 13
California, 16
Colorado, 16
copper, 6, 7, 8, 9,
       18, 19
crystals, 8

D

diamonds, 12

E

Egypt, 16, 20
Egyptians, 4, 20
elements, 6, 7, 8
Europe, 16

H

howlite, 18

I

Iran, 11, 16
Israel, 16

J

jewelry, 4, 18, 20

M

magnesite, 18
matrix, 10
Mexico, 16
minerals, 6, 12, 18
Mohs' scale, 12

N

Navajo Indians, 20
Nevada, 16
New Mexico, 16

P

phosphorus, 6, 7, 8

R

Romans, 16

S

sedimentary rocks, 6, 8

T

Tibet, 4
Turkey, 16
Tutankhamen, 20, 21

U

United States, 16
Utah, 16, 19

WEBSITES

Due to the changing nature of Internet links, PowerKids Press has developed an online list of websites related to the subject of this book. This site is updated regularly. Please use this link to access the list: www.powerkidslinks.com/gotw/turq